AUTHOR'S NOTE

*The stories in this book are about real people and real events. In some stories there are
a few imagined characters doing the kinds of things people would have done.*

*Each of the castles in this book can be visited. The Tower of London, Castel Sant'Angelo
and Osaka are crowded museums in the middle of cities. Chambord in the forest
and Neuschwanstein in the mountains are almost unchanged. Caernarfon, Bodiam
and Krak des Chevaliers are partly ruins, Chateau Gaillard more so.
Windsor Castle is still a royal residence.*

For Liz ~ S.B.

To Ben ~ M.H.

Numbers like this ◇ help you find your way around the pictures.
When you come across a number in the story, check where it appears on the small picture.
Then turn back the page to find your place on the big picture.